What others say about *Lord, Could You Make It a Little Better?*

"This promises to be one of the most frequently purchased gift books and one of the most widely quoted volumes of the year—and deservedly so!"
The Christian Century

"An inspirational volume for those who read reflectively. It deals with numerous human situations, problems, and aspirations. . . ."
Tampa, Florida, *Tribune*

"This is a beautifully written celebration of life as Robert Raines experiences it. Each poem is a window looking out upon a part of the world. Life's goodness is celebrated in people, in children, in family events, in a dozen other daily encounters. God speaks through these experiences and so does Raines."
The Messenger

"The reader will certainly find much to enjoy and relate to in this book. He will also find himself sharing the 'dreams, frustrations, and deeper yearnings' with a person he's never met, and thinking, 'That's how I sometimes feel.'"
The Jackson Sun

"This is a most attractive and unusual book. Not only does the material cover such varied subjects, but its design and format is unique and imaginative. Highly recommended!"
The Record

"A perfect bedside book for those occasional nights when the day's churnings won't leave you."
The Sacramento Union

LORD,
COULD YOU
MAKE IT
A LITTLE
BETTER?

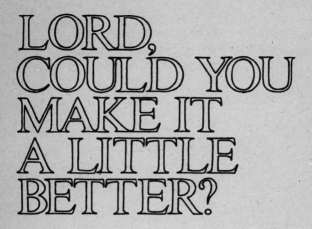

LORD, COULD YOU MAKE IT A LITTLE BETTER?

ROBERT A. RAINES

A Key-Word Book

WORD BOOKS, PUBLISHER
WACO, TEXAS

LORD, COULD YOU MAKE IT A LITTLE BETTER?
Designed and Illustrated by Bob and Sandy Bauer

LORD, COULD YOU MAKE IT A LITTLE BETTER?
By Robert A. Raines

First Key-Word Book edition May 1976

Copyright © 1972 by Word, Incorporated
Waco, Texas 76703

ISBN #0-87680-866-6
Library of Congress catalog card number: 76-188070
Printed in the United States of America

The quotation marked JB is from *The Jerusalem Bible*,
copyright © 1966 by Darton, Longman & Todd, Ltd.
and Doubleday and Company, Inc., and is used
by permission of the publisher.

To Peg

CONTENTS

PREFACE

I wish to express my deep appreciation to my wife, my parents, my children and friends who have called forth the yearnings in me which follow on these pages. The yearnings come out of our life together.

Many people have helped me in reflecting on these yearnings whom I would like to thank in this way. Among them are Matey Janata, John and Adrienne Carr, Jean Dones, and Floyd Thatcher.

I am also grateful to the congregation I serve, The First Community Church of Columbus, Ohio, for the generous provision of time to write this book.

August 1971
Glen Arbor, Michigan

ROBERT A. RAINES

INTRODUCTION

This summer I sat down many mornings and tried to let my yearnings come out on paper. I wrote down what I could of the feelings alive inside of me. It was a reflective time in my life—a change of jobs a year ago, a year of learning a new situation, a year of family adjustment, and some summer leisure in which to savor and distill what was going on. In the process of writing down my yearnings, I discovered more of who I am. I came to realize that our innermost longings and intuitions may remain hidden from other people, and more poignantly, from ourselves, unless we give some tangible expression to them.

The purpose of this book is to share some of my yearnings in the hope that you will be helped to get in closer touch with your own yearnings, to be more aware of those special moments of delight and wonder, to be more open to the beauty of a fleeting observation or feeling, to know what your own strange yearning feels like and looks like. A man who is making a decision about his job and future said to me, ''I am trying to listen to my insides. I don't want to deny what's going on there.'' I hope this book will help you listen to your insides and pay attention to what is going on there. God speaks to us through our neighbor, through history, nature, the Bible, and also from within. That inner voice is beginning to make sense to me, not as some sort of occult mystery, but as the stuff and depth of my own yearning.

Yearning is a significant form of prayer. Paul spoke of it in these words, "The Spirit helps us in our weakness; for we do not know how to pray as we ought, but the Spirit himself intercedes for us with sighs too deep for words" (Rom. 8:26, RSV).

I am told that I sigh a lot. Maybe you do, too. Sighing is an expression of our human weakness, the limitations of our existence, all that hems us in or walls us out or prevents us from reaching people we long to reach or from finding fulfillment. Sighing allows our inner longing to live and move. Paul assures us that God is in our sighing, even that it is his Spirit sighing in us and for us and with us and through us. God is at the heart of our deepest hoping and fearing. It is he who releases our yearning and allows it to come to the surface and pour out in stumbling words or silent tears. So we begin to pray when we yearn over our loved ones or enemies, our children and friends, the whole suffering world, the things and beings of nature, and our own selves.

Prayer is the outward yearning of my inward being. Whenever I am really seeing, hearing, touching, smelling, remembering, hoping with all my heart, I am praying. Some of us may think of God as a person out there, listening, caring, responding. Some of us may think of God as the power and spirit that holds all things together, sustaining, enabling, embracing. We try to name the silence and to see the face of the darkness, for we do not want to pour out our yearning into chaos or nothingness. So we reach into the silence and listen to the darkness and try to trust the source of all that is and remember to be amazed that there is something instead of nothing.

Prayer does not depend for its validity or authenticity

upon the use of approved religious language. Indeed, for some people, the spirit of prayer may be snuffed out by the use of such language. Use whatever words are natural and appropriate for you. Take hold of your yearning, see what comes out of you, and try to follow where it goes.

These fragments of my yearnings may possibly trigger your remembering and hoping, connect with your hunches, and provide signals of recognition. But you will want to express your own yearning, perhaps write it down. It may be amazing what happens when you take hold of the tip of your own yearning and just let it out on paper. Don't be surprised if you find yourself writing in poetic form. Everybody is a poet; you are. Poetry expresses feelings and intuitions more adequately than prose. It is no coincidence that the psalms, some of the most enduring prayers in human history, are written in poetic form and originally were to be sung. In fact, many hymns in poetic form are really singing prayers, prayers set to music. As the psalmist put it:

> deep is calling to deep
> > as your cataracts roar
> all your waves, your breakers
> > have rolled over me

> In the daytime may Yahweh
> > command his love to come
> and by night may his song be on my lips.
> > a prayer to the God of my life!
> > > —Psalm 42:7-8, JB

Sighs sometimes lengthen into songs, and yearning, like Zorba, turns to dancing. There's a yearning in you. Turn it on. Let it out.

THERE'S A YEARNING IN ME

there's a yearning in me
hidden in my sighs too deep for words
there's so much I feel
but don't understand
or even perceive
but it's there
all there
feelings, hopes, intuitions, fears, longings
and it all comes alive when I sigh

there's a yearning in me
to believe that the universe
is held together at the center
that there is somewhere in the whirling galaxies
to hang my hat and pin my hopes
a yearning in my restlessness that will not rest
a yearning in the meaningless rat race
to be and stand
a yearning to reach through all the walls
of death and hate
to shake hands with life and love
a yearning to belong, create, participate
and feel valued from the core of creation
a yearning to sing, in tragedy and through death
the praise of life

there's a yearning in me
a longing to let my sighs lengthen into songs
cascading through creation
ricocheting off the stars
echoing in human hearts and
resounding in my heart with a joyous Amen!

WAITING FOR A HUG

Lord, I keep thinking

about that seventeen-year-old girl

who told me her mother

hadn't hugged her

since she was in the

seventh grade—

What makes people

hold their hugs

back?

Is there someone

who's waiting

for a hug

from me?

WISDOM AND UNDERSTANDING

God of truth,

grant to all who teach

the wisdom to know

they are not wise;

and to all who learn

the understanding

that they do not understand.

Thank You

THANK YOU FOR WET LEAVES
WHICH TOUCH ME
WITH YOUR CONSTANT CARE
AS THE SEASONS COME AND GO
AND TIME GOES BY.

THANK YOU FOR WET CHEEKS
WHICH REMIND ME
THAT I MUST DEPEND UPON YOU
FOR ALL THAT IS PRECIOUS TO ME.

THANK YOU FOR DEATH
WHICH SETS A LIMIT TO PRIDE
OF NATION, RELIGION, POSITION,
THAT IN THE FACE OF DEATH
I MAY SEE THE FRAGILE BEAUTY
OF LIFE.

THANK YOU FOR LIFE
WHICH OFFERS ME DAYS
NEVER LIVED BEFORE,
THAT I MAY SPEND
AND NOT HOARD MY LIFE
AND CHOOSE JOY OVER PLEASURE,
PEACE BEFORE EASE,
TRUTH INSTEAD OF SAFETY
AND LOVE ABOVE ALL.

Be with Barbie
so far away
keep her in honor
and in health
let her relax away from us
and rejoice in her freedom
and miss us a little too . . .

Let distance
make room for love to expand in . . .
may letters
create bridges of understanding
over which love can walk at leisure . . .

Open up all the power of
Barbie's being
for her delight
and the world's amazement
and our joy . . .

Protect her
as she travels home
that we be destined
for laughter
and not for tears . . .

make room for love

I feel for parents
who can't do for their kids
what they want to do
what I can do for my kids

parents whose kids
      go to school buildings that are
          old and forbidding
      play in broken-glass alleys
      learn to be bitter soon and angry long
      watch other kids getting opportunities
          that will never come their way
             white kids
             rich kids
             healthy kids
                like my kids

Lord, if I couldn't do what is right
for my kids
I would be angry and hurt
and feel that something is wrong
somewhere
in this country
in this state
in this city

after dinner

after
dinner
in the big leather
      (really Naugahyde)
chair
reading stories to my boy . . .
      girls playing records
        loudly
      Peg telling me about her day
        insistently
      telephone ringing
        incessantly
on my way out of my mind
when
all at once
two tiny wet palms
on my cheeks
and
a small voice coaxing,
      "Look at me, Daddy, look at me!"

So
I look
and I see
      a beautiful boy face
      clear blue eyes
      yellow-brown hair
      on a perfect forehead
and it's like
Easter

Father,
my life is pulled into many directions
people clamor for my attention
my energies are dispersed
and I am stretched taut.

Help me to face
my limitations . . .

Pull me together
to an inner equilibrium
which can hold me steady
under pressure.
Grant me confidence
that the hands of fate or foe
sickness or sorrow
are your hands.

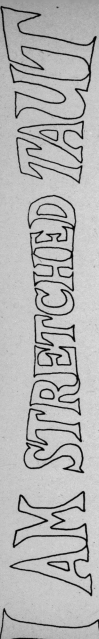

I AM STRETCHED TAUT

Into your hands
I commit
myself.

SHE'S DIVORCED

she's divorced, Lord
closed up with pain
determined never to be
vulnerable again
she's so hurt
bewildered and bitter
there he goes
to a new woman
a new life
here she stays
with the children
and the house
full of obligations
and an empty bed

she's lonely, Lord
gutsy
trying to get herself together
trying to be self-sufficient
without cutting herself off from people
trying to be tough
without getting hard
she's making it

I admire her
help me affirm her
as a human being
as a woman
without being misunderstood
without misunderstanding

KEEP ME VULNERABLE

O spirit within me
be my guide through all that is dark and
doubtful
be my guard against all that threatens my
honesty
be my strength under pressure and my
consolation in sadness
be my joy in celebration and
my comfort in disappointment . . .

let not success make me arrogant
but rather grateful
let not failure make me fearful
but rather wiser
let not pain or malice embitter me
but enlarge my capacity to endure
and to overcome
keep me vulnerable
to others
and so to
you

Break down the ancient enmities
and make peace
in our land

let the rich share power
let the poor take power
let the old advise and consent
let the young create and dissent
let us love the good in our country
more than we hate the evil

bring into the common life
all those who are left out
and who feel left out
give hope to all who have reason
to fear the future
give us passionate determination
to use the great wealth and power in our nation
that each child may live in a decent home
go to a first-class school
have opportunity for a job suitable to
his talent and skill
and that the aged shall abide in
security and dignity

deliver us from narrow affections
and partisan considerations
that our hopes be inclusive rather than
exclusive
and that our spirit be to share rather than to
hoard

restrain the reckless among us
and curb the violence in us all
that we may defend the weak
pursue justice without partiality
and conduct ourselves with
forbearance

that which is evil in us, let it die
that which is good in us, let it grow
until there is brotherhood from sea to shining sea
and we become in truth
as in hope
America the beautiful

AMERICA
THE
BEAUTIFUL

                                    O Lord
                          quiet my fears
                    and restore my hope

                I AM LONELY FOR YOUR TOUCH

                                    O Lord
                          quiet my fears
                    and restore my hope

I am lonely for your touch
        take me in your hands
        purge out of me the lurking grudge
        prune my self-will
        nourish in me a spirit supple to your leading
        root me deep in your peace
        sort out my tangled desires and duties
        save me from superficial involvements
        and scattered energies
you have filled my days with
        gladness of heart
        and taught me to sing
        songs in the night
you are the God of my hope and my fear
I love you
        and would love you more
let me savor joy
        and taste truth
        in the routine of my life
        and let it be holy to me
let not my zeal for peace flag
        nor my passion for justice be spent
        but let me work for peace
        and strive to make things more just

sit with me by the bedside
walk with me by the roadside
stand with me by the graveside
pray with me and for me
        in every moment's need
let me be wise but not cynical
        innocent but not foolish
        strong but not callous
        weak but not despairing
give depth to my speech
        and significance to my action

breathe your spring spirit
on my buried hopes
that my life may break forth
in wild color and rich beauty

throw open the windows of my house
that your salt breeze
may sweep through my stale habits

blow over the fences
of my self-pity
that I may run a race
against my low opinion of myself
and win

whisk away the blinders
of my gloom

spring your joy on me
and
waken me to wonder

SHE'S CRANING HER NECK

SHE'S CRANING HER NECK,
ALMOST BREAKING
TRYING TO FIND OU
WHO SHE IS . . .
IT LOOKS PAINFUL
THAT CRANING
TO SEE AROUND A HOPE
OR UNDER A FEAR
SOMETIMES I GUESS
A PERSON HAS TO TURN INSIDE OUT
TO GAIN SELF-KNOWLEDGE
I WISH IT WEREN'T SO
AWKWARD FOR HER
AND PAINFUL

HOW CAN I SAY TO HER
THAT I LIKE HER NECK
THE WAY IT IS?
RIGHT NOW SHE'S BEAUTIFUL
TO ME
SHE DOESN'T HAVE TO CRANE HER NECK
FOR ME

BUT THEN IT ISN'T FOR ME SHE'S CRANING
IT'S FOR HERSELF
SHE WON'T BE HAPPY
UNTIL SHE FINDS OUT FOR HERSELF
WHO SHE IS
EVEN IF SHE BREAKS HER NECK
CRANING

TAKE CARE OF THAT LOVELY NECK, LORD

I
THINK
ABOUT
PEOPLE

I think about people who work
in factories, shops, offices, kitchens,
executive suites, and mine shafts,
schools and churches and synagogues.
I think about artists and entertainers,
businessmen and brokers,
streetcleaners and streetwalkers,
sailors, soldiers, and flyers,
people who have something to do.

I think about people who don't work
because they're too old or too young,
too black or too ignorant or too sick,
people who don't know the right people
or were brought up on the wrong side of the tracks,
people who have nothing to do.

Father, I want to work
for a society in which
each shall give according to his ability
and receive according to his need,
in which we shall not use people and love things,
but love people and use things.

kisses in the air

I love
   getting up early
   the smell of morning coffee
   walking in the wet grass
   the morning paper . . .

I watch the children
   hurrying through breakfast
   racing out the door
   skirts flying
   kisses in the air . . .

There they go
   struggling out of the
   cocoon
   of my love . . .

Let me love them enough
   to let them go
   wisely, easily
let them fly far and high . . .

O Lord
bless our country and
our countrymen
    middle-Americans and middle-agers
    and everybody on all sides of
    every dividing line
    politicians and priests
    diplomats and ditchdiggers
    young men going places
    and all the girls who live next door

Restore our trust in one another
Renew our respect for diversity
Let us not confuse dissent
    with disloyalty
    nor patriotism
    with partisanship
Let us love America
    and change it
    and shape it
    until our alabaster cities
    are undimmed by human tears

Renew our confidence
    in the nobility of the dreams
    of our forefathers
    and our own
    while we acknowledge our mistakes
    and failures
Forgive us for pride in our own righteousness
    and believing that you are on our side
Staunch the tears of the angry poor
    and the blood of the Vietnamese
Turn our might to creation
    instead of destruction
Make us not wolves of prey
    seeking domination
    but people of peace
    seeking reconciliation

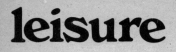

leisure

leisure is a blessing
to me and my family and friends
green meadows and
blue waters
are a healing sight for sore eyes
and sore selves
grant me the will
to savor my solitude
I want to look at the faces of the forest
and listen to the voices of the wind
I want to enjoy the silence
and the conversation
and to dig deep into the wells
of my own being
keep me from hurrying by
my life

leisure is a curse
to people penned up
in boredom, sickness, poverty, prison
time is terrible for those
who aren't going places
because they have no place to go
people pacing up and down
people shuffling in and out
people without a song
        without a job
        without a promise

Lord, grant me so to benefit from
my blessed leisure
that I may care more deeply for people
whose leisure is a curse

LOYALTY THAT LAID HOLD DEEP IN ME

Mother's Day
the phony commercialism
the shallow sentimentalism
I resent being directed
by ad men and con men
to appreciate a special person
by the numbers
on a date or day

But . . .

my mother
coming around the corner
seeing me in a fight
with another boy
not knowing whose fault
shouting from half a block away
Give it to him, Bob!
gloriously, blindly prejudiced
in my favor
what it means
to have someone
prejudiced in your favor
unconditional love

my mother
speaking in a contest
whether I won or lost
she thought I was the best
reality problems, pride problems
but what it means
to have someone
think you're the best
loyalty that laid hold deep in me

my mother
driving me on dates
when I was too young to have a license
having olives and peanuts
when I came home from college on vacation
because she knew they were a treat
for me
accepting my wife as a daughter
letting me go to be a husband
wanting to be remembered
appreciated, valued
sometimes hurt at being
taken for granted
not realizing that
she built into my bones
whatever confidence in myself I have
whatever capacity to trust
whatever strength of being

my mother
hidden health
of my life

I AM NOT A HERO

I admire heroes
but I am not a hero

I am struggling
to sort out
my small responsibility
from all that needs to be done
and
not to feel guilty
for not being
a hero

Is it false heroics
I'm feeling
          a desire for drama
          attention
or
is it a longing
to give myself
wholly
to something

something in me wants to risk
something in me wants to hold back

what will you do
with a both/and me?

Father

shield the children from my weaknesses
protect them against my attempts to
round them off or square them away . . .

let me understand them when they are
bearing burdens they cannot share with me
nor let me help carry . . .

let me not pry when I see them suffering
from sins unpublished
but deep with inner shame . . .

let them be brave and safe
but if they cannot be both
let them be brave . . .

let me share their tiny tragedies
and terrible heartaches
their soaring delights and
silent revelations
if they want me to
and as they want me to

let their confidence be established in
you . . .

SHIELD THE CHILDREN

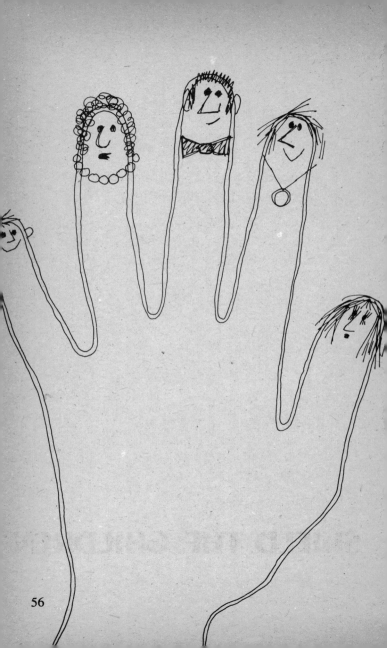

FACES AND HANDS

I love to remember those precious moments
when I saw people this week
really saw them
      the innocent glory of my child's face
      the lined faces of patient parents
      the unarmored face of one who knows
        he is dying
      the hands that heal
      the hands that caress
      the veined, hairy hands
        of work and love

why do I cause pain to those faces
      and make those hands go on guard?
why do I turn the knife
      belittle
      demean
      undercut
while I want to
      open the door
      build up
      appreciate
      encourage

let me bring light to those faces
and gentleness to those hands

THE VALLEY OF HUMILIATION

Lord Jesus
who rode into the city of man
before the stares of your enemies
and the shouts of your friends . . .

Grant me to gaze into your eyes
that my easy praise of you may be stilled
and my capacity to deny and betray be acknowledged
that in silence
my stony heart be ploughed up
in humiliation and hope . . .

Let this day find me vulnerable
as you were vulnerable
that rejection may not devastate me
nor defeat destroy me
but strip me of all pretension
and gird me with truth . . .

As you were gentle
with the strength of one
whose confidence was rooted in God alone
so grant me such strength in your purpose
that I be not swayed by the praise of men
nor overwhelmed by their blame
nor swerved by pleasure or profit
from the way of your judgment
in me and for me . . .

As you wept over the city of your fathers
because they wouldn't admit its injustice
grant me to weep over the city of my fathers
for those who are powerless
and those who will not exercise their power
but stand aside and say, I wish I could help
but I can't take leadership because of my position . . .

Grant me not to be ashamed of your shame
nor to be embarrassed by the taunts of cynics . . .

Let me walk with you
into whatever valley of humiliation is to be mine
in the certain hope
that every valley shall be exalted . . .

I Failed
Last
Night

I failed last night...

this man was hurting,
     aching for someone
     to listen
     and share his hurt...

but I was tired
     and uninterested
     and wanting to be left alone...

he didn't stay long...

that's not the first time
     I've turned off,
     refused to be reached...

and it's like
     I can see myself doing it,
     but I do it anyway...

because
     I don't have the energy to care
or
     do I often care
     for really loving reasons
or
     is my caring professional
or
     an investment upon which
     I expect return?

Lord, forgive me
     when I fail to care
     for any reason.

TRUSTING THE PROCESS

Things are going my way, Lord,
    and I'm feeling great
    and grateful . . .
Let my way be your way . . .
Let my strength enable the
    strength of my colleagues to grow . . .
Let my weakness not hinder others
    nor unduly discourage me.
I'm beginning to understand
    that every person is both
      strong and weak.
Help me be more able to recognize
    and affirm the strength of others.
Let the experience of my own weakness
    strip me down to truth.
Let my confidence not make me
    impatient with others
    or overbearing
    but willing
    to trust the process.

Trust God and Sin On Bravely

I have to decide Yes or No
and neither option seems wholly right
but there is no third possibility
not to decide is to decide
so I must decide one way
or the other . . .
either way
somebody gets hurt
there's no painless, pure way through
my hands are tied
there are limits and I've reached them
how can I justify what I have to do?
to the parties involved?
to myself?
to you?

I remember Luther's comment
Trust God and sin on bravely
that's a dangerous freedom
and a gracious responsibility
I could abuse either the freedom
or the responsibility

Lord, will you go with me
as I decide?
cover my inevitable sin with your grace
accept me
even when I'm unacceptable
let my Yes or No
be born out of
a brave trust

Gracious God, our Father,
who has set us in families that we be not alone
    nor lonely,
bless my congregational family
this day.

that we be not alone

Thank you for parents and grandparents
whose love was the climate of our childhood;
who fed us and forgave us day by day;
who hoped for us and prayed for us year after year;
who taught us to have confidence in the world,
    in ourselves, and you.
Grant us now to rejoice in our heritage,
and reconcile us to our forbears
that our days be fruitful and our hearts thankful.

Thank you for children and grandchildren,
the little babies who delight in your world
and drink in your strength and gladness.
Let their new life kindle our own,
that we, too, may wonder and learn,
and know again that all things are possible with you.

Thank you for sons and daughters
who seek nothing less than truth,
and will be content with nothing less than justice.
Let us rejoice in their hopes,
and be encouraged by their dreams;
and follow them gladly into your future.

Thank you for husbands and wives,
    brothers and sisters,
and all those whom we call friend;
those who love us with a love that will not let us go;
those who believe in us when no one else does;
who laugh with us in daylight,
and cry with us in darkness.
When we hurt each other, heal us.
When we are tired, give us rest,
    and a sense of humor,
    and a place to play.
This day let all grudges die,
kindness be born, and peace abide among us.

a house of your own

Everyone needs a house of his own
a place where he can be
alone
away from everyone else
with himself
to do his own special thing

A small girl made a house of h
a tablecloth over
just large enough for
her older brother determin
to break into his sister's hous
and was on his hands and knees
halfway in
when she bit him on the rear
her mother didn't punish her
because he had violated her just privacy
sometimes, Lord
it's O.K. to chew the other person out . . .

My father is retired
at his summer cottage
he has a study of his own
where on summer mornings
he goes to do his work
a man needs to get away from his wife
in the morning
and a woman needs her husband to get away
but when my brothers and I are there
Dad lets us use the study
to do our work
and he doesn't go there in the mornings
it's a real sacrifice
for a study is a place to work
and a place to work is important
to every man
especially to a man who is retired.

Lord
bless the young
and the old
and all of us in between
and let each of us
find in this life
a satisfying
house of his own

I'm a child playing hide-and-seek
        waiting for someone to find me
        and call my name
        and say, "You're it!"

And you did it, Lord!
You found me hiding
        in the silliest, saddest places,
        behind old grudges . . .
        under tons of disappointments . . .
        tangled up in guilt,
        smothered with success,
        choking on sobs that nobody hears.

You found me
        and you whispered my name
        and said, "You're it!"
And I believe you mean it . . .

And now maybe
        the silent tears can roll out of my throat . . .
        get wet on my cheeks . . .

And now maybe
        I don't have to play hide-and-seek any more.

PLAYING HIDE-AND-SEEK

THIS FRUITFUL SEASON

O Lord of the harvest moon
thank you for the time of yellow-red leaves
football games, cider, pumpkins,
fire-warm laughter, and the cheer
of this fruitful season.

Let it be a fruitful season
for my family, colleagues, friends and
for me.
Ripen us to maturity
    that we may come to terms with ourselves,
    bear one another's burdens,
    and forgive one another's mistakes.
Keep us from constant criticizing
    of those we love,
    lest our disapproval of them
    outshout our love for them
Let us be patient with each other
and, when I need to,
encourage me to put my arm around myself.

When we fail or lose or give up,
    let us not condemn
    but comfort each other
    and encourage each other
    to begin again.
Set us free from what has been
    and what might have been
to live for what may be.
Give us a hope, Lord,
    and restore to me a future.

REMEMBERING AND FORGETTING

O God I remember the children
who slurp their milk
crawl on the cool grass
stagger with their first hilarious steps
the eager children who play ball
and climb trees and ride bikes
eat hamburgers and ice cream
get in fights and play games
the laughing-crying kids
whose hugs and kisses and tears
are food and drink to me
      Let me not forget the children
      who have no milk to drink
      crawl on hot streets where there are no trees
      and see on TV how the other 80 percent live

O God I remember those in the prime of life
whose work prospers
whose families are happy
who eat the fruits of competence and achievement
who are glad to be who they are
who enjoy their leisure
and take their pleasure
who look back with satisfaction
and ahead with anticipation
    Let me not forget those whose work is frustrating
    who discover in themselves a wound
    which will never heal
    whose marriage hurts or breaks
    whose friends move away
    or fade away
    who wish they were somebody else

O God I remember those who are old
whose silver threads shine with honor
whose golden anniversaries sing with joy
whose children remember to write them
and telephone them and visit them
who have enough health and money
who have found wisdom
and learned patience
and journeyed in faith
    Let me not forget the old
    whose health fails
    whose children fail
    whose courage fails
    who must worry to their dying day
    about bills
    who languish forgotten in nursing homes
    or lonely apartments
    who feel unwanted and unneeded
    who have not found faith

happy birthday

Years ago
my father wrote me on my birthday:

Happy birthday, dear son.
You are a great joy to me.
I pray for your continued growth
to your measure of the stature
of the fullness of Christ.

> *To competitiveness*
> *add gentleness and sensitivity.*

> *To the will to win*
> *add the will to understand and comfort.*

> *To concern for the welfare*
> *of your own family and friends*
> *add concern for all who suffer*
> *and willingness to take your share*
> *of the suffering of mankind on your shoulders.*

> *To the will to make the most of your talents*
> *add the will to be the kind of husband*
> *and father who wants most to see his wife*
> *and children growing up towards the fulfillment*
> *of their talents.*

> *To impatience with inefficiency*
> *add the magnanimity which saves another's face*
> *and seeks for him open doors*
> *and at the same time can take responsibility*
> *and insist on change where necessary.*

May strength for every demand of life be yours.

SHOW ME A FEW TABLES

Lord, bring me back into focus.
    Wake me up.
    Fill me up.
    Connect me.
    Simplify me.
Make my step definite,
    and show me a few tables
    that need kicking over.

ON THE BEACH

on the beach
without my glasses
looking
appreciating

a gorgeous blonde
statuesque
blooming
ripe

coming toward me
shouting
laughing
reaching

O Lord ...
my darling daughter!

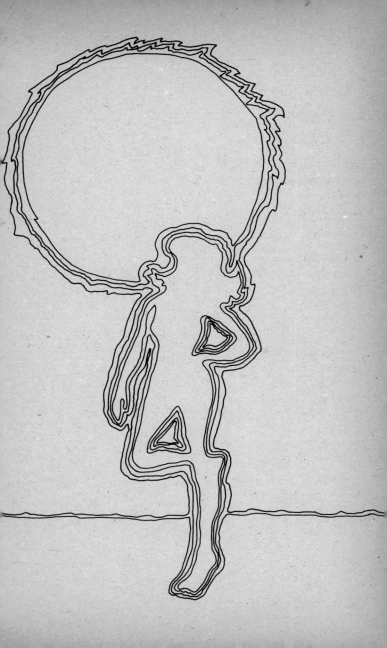

I LOVE YOU

SOMETIMES IT'S HARD
  TO TELL SOMEONE TO HER FACE,
  I LOVE YOU.
SOMETIMES IT'S EASIER
  TO SAY,
  GO TO HELL,
AND SLAM THE DOOR.

LORD, UNSLAM MY DOOR SO
  SHE CAN COME IN
  AND I CAN GO OUT . . .
UNSTOP MY EARS SO
  I CAN HEAR HER SIGHS AND SONGS
  AND MY OWN . . .
UNBLIND MY EYES SO
  I CAN SEE THE LONELY HUMAN BEING
  IN HER ANGER AND HURT
  AND MY OWN . . .

AND, FREE ME
  TO TELL HER TO HER FACE,
  I LOVE YOU.

what's wrong with you, lord?

The headlines hit me in the face again today
with who's happy and who's sad . . .

I'm glad for the happy ones:
   promotions, weddings, winning, making it big . . .
but there is so much sadness,
so much that doesn't need to be . . .
shouldn't be . . .
it's unfair, it's horrible!

How can you make a world in which
   people starve in Pakistan,
   nineteen-year-old boys kill each other in Vietnam,
   fire destroys a whole family in that tenement house?
Why, with all the new cars, trips, lobster, steak,
   gin and Scotch around,
   is there never enough money to give the city's children
   a decent education, or the poor a decent living standard?

What's wrong with you, Lord?
Can't you do something about it?

You mean . . . you expect ME
   to do something about it?

Oh . . .

Let Me Be
Like a Child
Surprised

Let me be like a child surprised to find another
    Easter egg hidden in a dark place ...

Trigger in me little explosions of
    wonder and delight ...
    push the buttons, pull out the stops,
    up with the windows, down with the walls,
    over with the fences of exclusion,
        and the tables of oppression ...
    out with demons of hate
    in with angels of love ...

Kindle in me fires of a strange surmise,
    and stir up wild dreams
        fantastic and stupendous,
    dreams of nations hugging each other across
        rivers and deserts and oceans ...
    dreams of a rainbow people holding hands
        around a city ...
    dreams of friends and enemies leaning
        over to kiss away the tears ...

Let me be like a child surprised ...

SOMEONE SENT ME A BIRTHDAY CARD

Someone sent me a birthday card
with a middle-aged boy scout
on the outside cover
spindly legs
spreading paunch
scouting paraphernalia
draped all over him
and a dejected look
on his futile face
underneath this wreck of a man
the words:
 At your age
and then on the inside of the card
the words:
 what's there to be prepared for?

Lord, you must have a sense of humor
to have made
people
You can't be all business
There must be a laugher
hidden in the heart of creation

Let me laugh at myself
and not take myself too seriously
Let me make judicious use of my energies
and maximize the benefits of experience

and let me consider
at my age
what I am preparing for

I'm forty-five today
looking back on forty
and ahead to fifty
we've spent too much money
on other things lately
to have much left for birthday presents
but my gifts are already in hand

I'm content on my forty-fifth birthday
there's much yet I want to do
and more I want to be
but I'm content
not satisfied with myself
nor totally fulfilled
nor without dreams of tomorrow
        or regrets from yesterday
but content
today

And grateful
twenty-one years together with Peg
she's in town now
shopping, planning with children
and friends
for the celebration tonight
when she left for town
I reached over to hug her and
look at her and kiss her
she asked me what I was thinking
and I said nothing special

How do you speak of forty-five years alive
and twenty-one years together?

Lord, I want to see around the corner
but all I really need
is light enough to take the next step
give me that light

Forgive me for taking credit
for my colleague's idea
and blaming him
for my mistake

Renew our affection for one another
in the family
help me respect the feelings of the children
and let their responses to me come naturally
that I not coerce them, even gently, to respond the
way I want them to
help me set limits on bad language and behavior
while encouraging the freedom to express
anger and hate feelings

Let my friendships be inclusive
and let me not be jealous
of the other friendships
of my friends

Keep me from crossing that man off my list
and show me how and when and where
to receive his hostility hopefully
give me the guts to say "I'm sorry"
and the grace to say "It's O.K."

Let the strength of my conviction
be matched
by the depth of my respect for
another's conviction

Let my reciting of the Lord's Prayer
and asking for daily bread
take the form of working
for justice in my city
that I may practice what I pray

Let me be glad for all that is good in me
while I struggle against what is evil
bless those who suffer because of the sins of others
judge those who profit from the sufferings of others
bless me
judge me

Come, Lord Jesus,
come into our divided world
tense this night in uneasy truce;
come, and give us your peace.

Come into our divided nation,
tense this night in the apathy of the rich
and the bitterness of the poor,
torn with tension between those who are content
and those who are discontent;
come, and give us your peace.

Come into our divided homes,
tense this night with angry words
and crying faces,
torn with tension between what could be
and what is;
come, and give us your peace.

Come into our divided hearts,
tense this night with desire to be
vindicated
and to be forgiven;
come, and give us your peace.

Come, Lord Jesus,
on this your natal night;
come, and give us your peace.

COME, LORD JESUS

All My Loves

LET YOUR LOVE
HEAL AND HALLOW
ALL MY LOVES

QUIET THE DRUMBEAT OF DESIRE
SEVER THE SOFT CHAINS
OF SELF-INDULGENCE

YOUR GRACE COMES TO ME
ON THE WINGS OF MY PARENTS' PRAYERS

I AM PETTY, LORD,
GIVE ME MAGNANIMITY
I AM STRAINING, LORD,
GIVE ME CONFIDENCE

PACIFY MY UNRULY PASSIONS
REALIGN MY DEFLECTED PRIORITIES

I WANT TO TASTE YOUR TRANQUILLITY
AND DRINK YOUR HEALTH

CHRISTMAS IS COMING

Christmas is coming!
and it's the time of children again,
wide-eyed wonders and
whispered secrets,
greens and wreaths,
crèches and candles,
cards at the door,
carols in the air,
snowflakes on hot chimneys,
and questions parents can't answer:
    "Why can't dogs laugh?
    Why is snow cold?
    Why is Jesus' birthday?"
       O, let us old ones be like
       children again.

Christmas is coming!
and there are so many lonely people;
soldiers lonely for home,
the Vietnamese people lonely for peace,
refugees, prisoners, the starving, and
outsiders lonely for food and power.
We are lonely, Lord,
lonely for loved ones whose chair at
        the table is empty this Christmas,
lonely for children who have grown up
        and gone away,
        and for those who haven't
        yet really let us into their lives,
lonely for parents who understand,
lonely for a Currier and Ives world
        which is no more,
        and for a peaceful world
        which is not yet.
You know what it is to be lonely, Lord,
        there in a manger, no room in the inn,
        there on the road, no place to lay your head,
        there on a cross, no one to save you.
            O, let us lonely ones find
            one another again.

Christmas is coming!
and there's so much to do, buy, remember
only nine shopping days left,
the trash collector,
postman, milkman, neighbors, relatives, friends,
family,
time running out, money running out,
patience running out,
things get in the way of people—
but wise men watch and wonder,
    and pause to look for the stars
    in people's eyes
        and to listen for angel-singing
    in the night.
        O, let us busy ones wise up
        and watch for joy again!

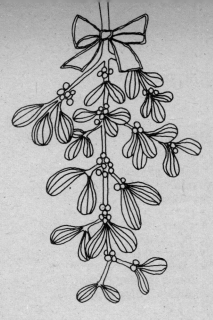

Christmas is coming!
and it's the time for giving
and forgiving,
but we get so mad so fast about
so little, and sometimes
it's hard to remember
how to be happy,
        and we hug our hurts
        instead of each other.
But Lord, Christmas is coming,
and we want to smile and laugh and dance,
so, please, tease away our frowns,
and let the mistletoe appear above every
head, and
kiss away our tears, and make us
huggers and lovers,
givers and forgivers,
children of all ages!
Come on, Jesus, light our fires!

I'M LONELY ON THIS JET

I'm lonely on this jet . . .
    away from my family
    and my home . . .

      only a few days, but
      I feel disconnected, anonymous,
        like a missing person,
      does anybody miss me?

     out the window there
        are those airport lamp lights
        bending over gently, but
        their lights do not comfort me . . .

        most of the time I feel self-sufficient . . .
        maybe I take for granted
           the affection of my family
           and fail to realize how much
           I depend upon them
           for my security and comfort . . .

sometimes I'm alone and
    not lonely . . .
but now
 I'm lonely on this jet . . .

BLOOD ON

OUR HANDS

O God, whose compassion is upon the powerless
and whose anger is upon the heartless . . .

We sit here in this country with blood on our hands
and all we can think to do is wring these bloody hands.
Forgive our complacence with killing.
Rebuke our shrugs at poverty and war
as though we could do nothing about them.
Confront us who can feed and protect our own children
that we rest not till all parents can feed and
protect their children.
Save us from the fever of lusting after victory
and the destruction of the enemy.
Grant us to care more about saving lives than saving face.

Let us love our country not less
but mankind more
in the knowledge that
a nation is great in your eyes
when it feeds the hungry,
welcomes strangers,
rehabilitates those in prison,
heals those who are sick,
and treats the least of these
as though they were the most.

Time To Believe and Hope Again

It's time!
time to believe and hope again!
make it spring in my wintered body,
bring me out of hibernation,
see the sun, Lord, see that new sun,
breaking its own record for smiling,
feel its warmth and you smile, too,
and I'll smile with you.

Hey, look at that new world stirring,
cracking loose from the ice,
surfacing in yellow, violet, and pure gold.
listen to all those crazy birds,
fantastic orchestra without a conductor!
I'm eager for the return of the robin,
stretching to be surprised
by a dream or even a duty.

You're calling me out
of my cold prison
into your warming world,
and I'm hearing
and I'm coming out,
for it's time,
time to believe and hope again!

YANK ME OFF THE TREADMILL OF SELF-PITY

yank me off the treadmill of self-pity

pull me out of my failure into your future

I'm a prisoner of my own needs

and fed up with chasing empty illusions . . .

woo me to a new way

catch me off guard with forgiveness

stub my toe on your patience

free me from the tyranny of wanting approval . . .

dust me off

save me
  from aimlessness
  mean ambition
  cheap pleasure
  empty leisure

and thank you
  for strength I didn't know I had
  for confidence when things didn't go my way
  for not going to pieces when everything got shaky

and when I'm feeling sorry for myself again

because I've struggled much and achieved little

then I'll turn to you for another

  yank . . .

I'M A CLOWN

I'M A CLOWN
HUNCHED DOWN IN A LITTLE RED CIRCUS CAR
WAITING FOR SOMEONE TO OPEN THE DOOR
AND LET ME OUT—

AND YOU DID IT, LORD . . .
YOU OPENED MY DEATH'S DOOR
    AND HERE I COME
LAUGHING THROUGH MY TEARS . . .
SHOUTING PAST MY FEARS
JUMPING OVER WALLS . . .
    RIDING HIGH—
    LOOK, LORD, NO HANDS!

AND THERE GO THE BALLOONS—
    RED-SPLASHED,
    YELLOW-STREAKED,
    GRACIOUS GREEN,
    POLKA DOT AND PEPPERMINT—
LIKE A RAINBOW EXPLODING IN THE SKY . . .
LIKE FOURTH OF JULY AND CHRISTMAS AND
    EASTER ALL ROLLED INTO ONE GREAT
    WHOOPING
    YES

Riding Home in the Car

Riding home in the car
we don't say much
she's lost in thoughts
of her ballet
and I'm enjoying
just having her beside me

I look at her
looking out the window
her face is grave
in quiet repose
whatever she does is graceful
she's always pirouetting around the house
the budding ballerina
body slender but strong
surprising muscles in her calves
neck erect, head proud without pride
girl becoming woman
like a Greek goddess

She's my princess
and I love her
beside me
riding home in the car

FOR NINE YEARS NO SEX

For nine years
in that marriage
no sex

the enormity of it
denying
and being denied
for nine years

nine years of
sadness, hurt, rejection, loneliness
nine years of dehumanization
wasting, withering
dying

Lord, why do people accept death
in life so long
without cracking the cancer open?
is it too late for them?
can they retrieve nine years?
can they live again
together
or must they break apart
to live again?
help them choose to live
whatever it does to their marriage

keep me from accepting death
in my relationships
at home
and at work

is there someone whom
I'm denying, crippling, killing?

is there someone who is
cutting me down with neglect?

Lord, give me courage to choose life
whatever the conventional cost

HER FACE IS HARD TO LOOK AT

Her face is hard to look at
disfigured by surgery
cancer in the jaw
spreading
seventeen years old
she was a beautiful girl

at first she was bitter
but now she's making plans
going to college
while the cancer
eats into her lungs

she's brave, stoic
and so are her parents
they don't want pity
they don't seem to feel
sorry for themselves
but they know it's only a matter of
time and pain
they're suffering
day by day
glance by glance

Lord, help them
and me face death head-on
I remember a man once said
"I don't want to be cheated of my death"
He was saying he wanted to
experience his death wide awake,
drink its taste to the full
I don't know
Lord, help them
and me look for death's meaning
death makes life
so precious
death can draw
a broken family together
death strips away the trivial and false
and reveals what matters

Lord, let life now
for her and her family
be rich with insight and love and self-revelation
give them in their time together
amazing grace
that they may know in this time
the secret joy of the time to come

swimming into the waves

spray in my eyes
salt in my mouth
strength in my arms

I claim my own body

I exult in my body's strength
and reach out fierce
arm over arm
rolling, turning
drumbeat kicking
ploughing through the waves
I delight in my body

thrusting through burning sun
rolling sea
stinging salt

with my whole body I say
Yes

SWIMMING INTO THE WAVES

TILL ENEMIES BECOME FRIENDS

Be with those who are passionately seeking change
in our society, and with those who are angrily
resisting change, that we may respect one
another even as we work in diverse ways for
peace on earth and good will among men.

Be with those who languish in nursing homes,
and be with all of us in homes where grudges
are nursed; let grudges be gone and
friendship restored and suspicion give way
to trust.

Forgive that heady humanity which allows us
to care about people suffering across the city
or the ocean, but leaves us cold to the need
of those across the table or the desk.

Melt our cynicism with the hope of Jesus
and take us by surprise
with a near-forgotten intuition
stirring deep within us.

Shake us loose from patterned behavior
to love each other
without calculation or condition.

Break down our defenses
and lower our guard,
that for these brief days
we may be defenseless before you,
vulnerable as children,
ready for miracles,
eager for surprises,
till enemies become friends
and there comes
peace on earth and good will among men.

I'm all mixed up

I'm all mixed up
there's a multitude in me
    a smiler and a cryer
    a laugher and a listmaker
    a reconciler and a fighter
    a schemer and a dreamer
Who are we
in me?

Treat me tender, Lord
for all my bluff
I'm sore inside
and afraid sometimes
Sit with me in my shadows
dance with me in my sundance times
It's strange but
I'm often hurting most
when I'm telling jokes

I want to be so much more than
I am
I want to grow and change
and change things that should be changed
I want to hang on to what I've got
but I want everyone to have enough
I think I'm willing to be taxed
to make it happen

Forgive me for doing nothing
when I could do something
Forgive me for doing little
when I could do more
Forgive me when I acquiesce in prejudice
by saying nothing
or looking the other way
or pretending not to see or hear

Lord, you know me as I really am . . .
that comforts me
and
sobers me

O Spirit of all being
I search for you
in myself
Am I empty that you should fill me?
Am I afraid that you should comfort me?
Am I discontent that you should give me purpose?

I search for you
in my brothers and sisters
and see many
hurrying towards death unaware
Are you hurrying with them
to meet them at the door
or stop them on the way?

I search for you
in Jesus
and see a man
such as I would be
and a spirit
such as I would have you breathe

Are you searching
for me
through him
O Spirit of all being?

SEARCHING

I HAVE TO DECIDE

I delight in my being
when light floods in
and confidence
chases
darkness
away

yet
darkness comes in again
like fog
and I am groping
to find my way
I have to decide
and I can't know for sure
so I must decide in the
dark

are you with me in the dark?
will you go with me
whatever I decide
even if I am wrong or foolish or weak?
Lord, do you still choose me
when I choose something else
something less?

teach me to wait
in the silence
and trust
in the darkness

GIVE ME A GOOD EYE

Give me a good eye
to see all the cartoons people make
by being alive . . .
to delight in the vigor of young people
out to make the world,
and the twinkle in the eye of an old man
who remembers the good young days . . .

Thanks for those who love me
in the common ways of a smile,
a letter, a phone call,
and all the gentle touches
of hand and heart . . .

Thanks for those who confront me
with anger, hurt, pain,
and remind me that I don't always see them
as I go by . . .

If in pleasure we have gone our separate ways,
in pain draw us together.

THANKS for the MEMORIES

thanks for the memories that flood my heart
and sometimes my eyes

thanks for grandparents
    I heard the children singing the other night
    He's got grandpas and grandmas in his hands
    grandparents are another layer of special people
    for the children

thanks for loyal friends and colleagues
who forgive me
both my failures
and my successes

thanks for work to do
energy and skill to do it
enough money to support my family
and a place in the community

thanks for the smell of wet leaves yesterday
I love to walk in the woods
and smell the rain

thanks for my body
and her body
and all those words made flesh
and the sighs too deep for words

thanks for the mystery of my own being
I don't know who you are
or even whether you are
but I keep hoping
you are the Spirit of Jesus
in all humanity
and in me

WE ARE LOST

we are lost in a land of luxury
where nothing satisfies any more

there is no taste in mouths full of
the cake of affluence
but unwilling to provide
the bread of justice

there is no joy in hearts
open to private pleasure
but closed to public need

there is no laughter in ears
choked with chatter
but deaf to the cries of human suffering

I pray for our family . . .

help us acknowledge
the resentments that divide us
and the love that unites us
let us be slow to criticize
and quick to appreciate
slow to justify ourselves
and quick to excuse one another

when we disagree or misunderstand
let us listen to each other
and make out your truth
together

when we are tempted to betray each other
let us resist and endure
and if it may be
set us free from every desire and deed
that would devastate others
and cripple ourselves
and if it may not be
set us to picking up the pieces
of our broken promises
and trying to put ourselves
together again

when we fail
let us not wallow in self-sorrow
but grasp us in our angry pain
that we take up our failure and walk

in grief
let us put our arms around each other
in joy
let us sing and laugh and dance together
in life
let us celebrate our health
in death
let us celebrate our hope

winning an argument

a woman cried,
I haven't won an argument with my husband
in twelve years

that's a long time
she's a strong woman
her husband must be stronger
     or insensitive
     or insecure
     or out of touch with himself

when I'm in touch with my inward being
I experience the flow of insecurity there
and the chaotic improbability of life
and I know there is little I know for sure

what makes me insist I'm right
to make a point or win an argument?
I think it's needing to feel valued
for being right
because I don't feel valued just for being me
right or wrong

there's winning arguments
and exchanging opinions
and sharing ideas
and respecting convictions

there's a tight, taut self-sufficiency
which has a hard time admitting it's wrong
and denies a healthy dependence
on another

Lord, in my marriage
let Peg and me
make
a declaration of interdependence

O God, whose son Jesus did not fear to go into
    the city where he would be murdered,
save us in the congregation from fear
    of facing the dangers that confront us in our city.
Give us courage to pick up our murdered hopes
    and begin again.
Bless those who face pain, disappointment, and death,
    that they find hope in you.
Comfort those who are in bereavement,
    and let us receive with thanksgiving
    the benefits of those who have died.

O God, whose son Jesus made himself vulnerable
    to take common cause with children,
    the weak, the poor, the outsider, the unpopular;
awaken in us compassion for all who struggle
    against the odds.
Nourish in us the capacity to bear insult and
    forbear injury, knowing our own aggressions,
    and seeking ever to understand rather than to provoke.
Make us tender through suffering
    and generous through loss.
Help us so to value each person among us
    for who he is rather than what he does
    that we may live together without envy or malice
    and grow in affection with glad trust.

O God, whose son Jesus put himself in jeopardy
    to make a daring dream come true,
grant us in the common ventures of our time and place
    to be daring in action,
risking our investments,
and investing ourselves
for the sake of the future
in honor of the past
and to fulfill the present.

Facing
the
Dangers

MIDDLE-AGERS ARE BEAUTIFUL

Middle-agers are beautiful!
    aren't we, Lord?

I feel for us
    too radical for our parents
    too reactionary for our kids

    supposedly in the prime of life
        like prime rib
        everybody eating off me
           devouring me
        nobody thanking me
          appreciating me

    but still hanging in there
        communicating with my parents
        in touch with my kids

    and getting more in touch
        with myself

and that's all good

    thanks for making it good,

and

    could you make it a little better?

my Dad told me

     he and Mother look

     in the mail box

     every day.

I don't write very often

     even though I know

     how hungry they are

     to hear from me.

I pray for them often

     but don't write much . . .

better I should pray less

     and write more?

         or

         maybe

a letter

is a prayer

that meant what it said.

LOOKING IN THE MAILBOX

PEOPLE WHO DON'T SEEM TO NEED PEOPLE

People who need people
  are the luckiest . . .

I feel for people
  who don't seem to need people . . .
People who have made it
  or have it made,
  who are wondering
    if there's anything more . . .
    or if it's just more of the same
    from here on out . . .
People who are cool and competent,
  whose shyness comes through
  as aloofness or arrogance . . .
People who are worth a lot
  but don't feel worthy . . .
  who are lovely
    but feel unloved . . .
  who are valuable
    but feel unvalued . . .
People who wonder if their success
  covers emptiness inside . . .

Is it I, Lord?

LORD
I WANT TO GET OUT
GET AWAY
GET LOST
I CAN'T STOP RUNNING
TALKING, AVOIDING

HOLD ME STEADY
GIVE ME STAMINA
QUIET ME
TEACH ME
TO KNOW YOU
IN MY STILLNESS

YOU ARE
MY INNER EYE
OF UNDERSTANDING
YOU ARE
MY INNER HAND
OF TOUCHING
YOU ARE
MY INTIMATE DRUMMER
SOUNDING
MY REVEILLE
YOU ARE
MY QUIETNESS
AND
MY CONFIDENCE

MY INTIMATE DRUMMER

CHILDREN MAKE ME WONDER

Thank you for children,
    their trucks, dolls, questions, hugs,
    tears, giggles, games.

Children make me tender again
and make me wonder:

    about children in Pakistan and India
    without food—
        I picture my own children starving . . .

    children in Vietnam and our city's ghettos and suburbs
    without a father—
        I picture my own children orphaned . . .

    children starved for affection or
    orphaned of opportunity in our own community—
        I picture my own children poor . . . .

Sometimes the suffering of children
almost breaks my belief in you . . .

Lord, we exult in the early morning birdsong
which wakens us to green beginnings
and multicolored hopes
and pulls us to our feet
to stand on tiptoe
Surprise us with joy in the morning
struggle with us in heat of noonday
sit with us in the evening shadows of
    quietness and confidence
for you meet us at every corner
and bring new life out of all our dying
and create us ever and afresh
    a springtime people
    with Easter in our eyes

Bless our families
Let husband and wife be tender to each other
let the guard drop and the tears fall
and the heart open and the arms go round
Let parents and children listen to each other
and cry for each other
and laugh with each other

Easter in Our Eyes

Bless our friends
Thank you for weaving us together into a
fabric of friendship, a living tapestry of
glad/sad colors forever separating and uniting
You have made of us together
more than we were apart
You have bound us deep in the mystery of
death and birth
You have driven us in conflict
to cry out for help and healing
Forgive us all the ways in which we have
hurt or hindered one another
Reach deeper than self-pity or
self-justification
to forgiveness which yields
the love that bears, believes, hopes, endures
all things

Lord, we are uneasy looking into the future
we need to know that you are with us
and we are with you
Give us the confidence that though all things change
You are the same God
    ever gracious
      from whose love nothing can separate us
Let us feel you on our pulses
and in our breathing
and convince us in our very bodies
that we live and die
in the hollow of your hand
Release now those mute longings
hidden in our hearts
to join the early morning birdsong
singing green beginnings
and multicolored hopes
      for you are shaking us and
        shaping us into
        a springtime people
        with Easter in our eyes

A THREAD OF LIFE

you have made me
a creature of dust and divinity
and granted me a thread of life
you have covered the earth with living things
and spangled the skies with stars and suns
hanging in the dark silence

I don't know what to make of you

There's a yearning in you . . .
let it out

There's a yearning in you . . .
                    write it here

This is your page . . . why not use it?

For your yearnings

For your yearnings

OTHER BOOKS BY ROBERT RAINES

To Kiss the Joy

Robert Raines shares with us his deep awareness of the painfulness of growth, his yearning for the comfort of yesterday, and his sense of fear when faith is threatened. He urges us to live boldly, immediately; to live in unison with our dreams and dare to risk. #80324 (hardback).

Success Is a Moving Target

What does it mean to be a success—a successful person, a successful Christian? How do we measure success in a congregation or in a nation? Dr. Raines applies biblical insight and extensive personal experience to help us bring our ideals and realities together and to move from a ''right/wrong'' perspective to a ''sin and forgiveness'' perspective. #80395 (hardback).

Living the Questions

What do you do with the unsolved questions in your life? Robert Raines calls us to live them, as possibly a more realistic and faithful style of Christian living than looking for answers. The reality is that we live by faith, not by certainty or security. And faith implies questioning. His own personal questions openly shared with us, in poetry and prose, invite us to name and live our own questions. #80437 (hardback).

For more books to grow with . . .
please turn the page.

FOR FURTHER READING

Prayers from Where You Are. *Francis A. Martin.*

A sensitive collection of prayers from the heart. They are personal, yet they speak a universal language because they come from deep within the soul. Each prayer has a spontaneity about it that makes it fresh and relevant for today. #98035 (paperback).

Bread for the Wilderness/Wine for the Journey.
John Killinger.

Out of his own pilgrimage, John Killinger shares with us the deeper meaning of prayer and the inner life, and his own growing conviction that prayer is real. He helps us learn to be more attuned to the things of the spirit and the mystery of God's leading. #80443 (hardback).

All You Lonely People/All You Lovely People
John Killinger.

Who of us dares to admit our loneliness? John Killinger found the courage to share himself and his loneliness in a small caring group to which he and his wife belonged for a few months. A look at how a small group can become the body of Christ—with life-changing results.
#80315 (hardback).

Eighth Day of Creation. *Elizabeth O'Connor.*

After we have accepted ourselves, and have found that place where we can hear God speak to us, then we are called upon to act. God himself calls us to join the creative forces in the world by discovering our own creativity and gifts. Knowing who we are means that we acknowledge what it is our gift to do. Excerpts from other authors provide material for meditation. #80260 (hardback).

Search for Silence. *Elizabeth O'Connor.*

A marvelous book for helping us get in touch with our real self—that inner reality we so often neglect, ignore, or push away. With realism, Miss O'Connor helps us face our two-sidedness, and then calls us to prayer and contemplation—and to action. Excerpts from other authors provide further material for reflection and meditation. #80264 (hardback).

Peace with the Restless Me. *Janice Hearn.*

A real-life pilgrimage from futility to fulfillment. Janice Hearn lets us see her struggle to overcome depression and bitterness from the past, and shows us what she has learned of the resources God gives us through the Holy Spirit to become new persons in Christ. #80455 (hardback).

Dare to Be You. *James R. Dolby.*

An adventure in self-discovery, *Dare to Be You* is a springboard for fresh thinking and lively discussion in various areas of religious experience and daily life. The section ''As the Twig Is Bent'' traces the emotional and spiritual growth of the child from birth through the college years. #91005 (Key-Word paperback).

Yes Is a World. *James W. Angell.*

A rousing welcome into the life of affirmation. This hope-filled book includes chapters titled: Man Is Born with

Rainbows in His Heart; Not the Postponed Life; Transcendence Is a Kiss on the Nose; Instructions for Erecting a Tent in a Rainstorm; Yes Got Up Before the Sun; Dancing on a Battlefield. #80387 (hardback).

The Gift of Wholeness. *Hal L. Edwards.*

The warmly human story of a modern pilgrim in search of himself . . . and in search of God. A refreshing look at one minister and his ministry—a vulnerable, open kind of life that grows and keeps on growing. #80377 (hardback).

Barefoot Days of the Soul. *Maxie D. Dunnam.*

Remember when you were a child how you longed for the first warm days of spring when your mother finally let you go barefoot? How marvelous and free it felt. ''Nothing in my experience,'' says Maxie Dunnam, ''is more suggestive of the promise of the gospel than that. This book is about freedom. It's a thank-you celebration—an invitation to barefoot days of the soul.'' #80432 (hardback).

The One and Only You. *Bruce Larson.*

People don't come in carbon copies. We may accept that idea, but how do we make the most of being one of a kind? Bruce Larson is convinced that every one of us unique ''yous'' has an unlimited potential to draw on—the liberating security of God's love. Here he probes what that can mean for us and gives us practical ways of putting our potential to work. #91012 (A Key-Word paperback).

Let God Love You. *Lloyd John Ogilvie.*

In thirty-eight devotional meditations, the author takes the struggles of life seriously and turns them into stepping stones to Christian growth. Paul's letter to the Philippians forms the basis for these refreshing thoughts. #80353 (hardback).

The Becomers. *Keith Miller.*

A helpful and insightful look at what happens to a person after he or she becomes a Christian. Realistic, honest, and full of hope, for people who "are in the process of becoming whole as we reach out with open and creative hands toward work, people, and God."
#80321 (hardback).

Habitation of Dragons. *Keith Miller.*

"Miller is forceful, witty, honest and surprising in his interpretation of a Christian life style. [Here] we have a combat diary for people trying to enlarge on the spiritual dimensions of existence"—David Poling, *New York Times.* Divided into forty-two selections, *Habitation of Dragons* is a book to be lived with one day at a time. #80182 (hardback). #91010 (A Key-Word book).

Come to the Party. *Karl A. Olsson.*

An invitation to a celebration of life. God invites us to his party, but some of us are like the older brother—we look on from the outside, knowing the party is not for us—we are not free to accept the love and blessing of our Father. Learn with Karl Olsson how to enter into a freer life style, secure in the love of God. #80296 (hardback). #98001 (paperback).

Enjoy the Journey. *Lionel A. Whiston.*

Accepting the fact that God loves us in spite of our failures, understanding our fellow man, and facing up to moral responsibility are just a few of the keys to a fuller spiritual life which Lee Whiston discusses in his warm and personal way in this helpful book. #80250 (hardback).

The Edge of Adventure: An Experiment in Faith.
Keith Miller and *Bruce Larson*.

Discover the difference Christian commitment can make in your job and your vocation; in your involvement in the church; in overcoming guilt, fears, anxiety, loss of faith, loneliness, depression. Life can become an adventure. #98026 (paperback); #40088 (leader's guide); #40089 (study guide); CRC-0627 (13-week cassette study course).

Living the Adventure: Faith and Hidden Difficulties.
Keith Miller and *Bruce Larson*.

For Christians who are already ''beyond the edge'' and are now striving to live the adventure. Honest but hopeful insight into the difficulties that are part of living as a Christian—confession and forgiveness, money and possessions, Christian sexuality, loneliness, success, change and growth, sickness and death, and more. #98055 (hardback); #40103 (leader's guide); #40104 (study guide); CRC-0633 (13-week cassette study course).